AF504425

TABLE OF CONTENTS

YOU are AWESOME! You know this!

You could be doing so many other things right NOW, but YOU are smart enough + LOVE yourself enough to want to make YOU better, not just for yourself but for the people around you! Congratulations to YOU on being so wise and putting yourself in the driver's seat, please pat yourself on the back (no, really, please do it now, you deserve it)!

Imagine where you will be! Whether you want a beautiful retirement, you want to become a market professional, or you just want a few extra dollars in your pocket, you're in the RIGHT place, and I'm excited for YOU. My students have been doing AMAZING, and they helped inspire me to write this book for YOU. I am honored to have you as a reader and I promise to take good care of you, as I do with all of my students. You can take my courses whenever you are ready, and consider this book your first step forward! You are GREAT!

Thank you, Thank you, THANK YOU for wanting to learn and better yourself. You inspire me and I look forward to your growth and success. YOU GOT THIS!

Much Love, y con mucho cariño, merci beaucoup
Uch Anyanwu

1 - GET A MENTOR

Do YOURSELF a favor and Get YOURSELF a mentor!

When YOU were a baby, YOU didn't learn how to walk by YOURSELF, YOU had

guidance. YOU probably didn't learn how to drive on YOUR own either (1 of my students has by the way, so if that's you too, then God bless and congrats)!

Being your own teacher is admirable, but it is also the LONG road. When you're smart enough to leverage someone else's expertise, YOU will get further FASTER and with less pitfalls & headaches.

2 – DIVERSIFY

YOU Can Mix It Up !!!

Rather than putting your faith in 1 stock or sector and hoping for the best, you may

want to pick a few stocks in different sectors, and even things out (this is called "spreading your risk").

Some investors believe in going "ALL IN" on 1 stock, but when you do this you're putting yourself at a greater risk,

especially if the stock and/or sector fails to succeed.

When you have 5 or more blue chip stocks, spread across different appreciating sectors, and evenly weighted within your portfolio, you're setting yourself up for success and the ability to sleep at night.

3 – SELL THE NEWS !!

YOU'RE Better off when YOU
BUY the Rumor & SELL the News !!

You see so many people buy into a stock when a big news story hits the financial news, and even

the mainstream news. More times than not, this is the time YOU are supposed to SELL!

Be careful when buying into a stock on a news event, especially when you see a big run up to coincide with the news, often times the "smart money" is selling into this news event because they've been in the stock since the "rumor" when they bought in. Think of a "rumor" as news of a company idea that has not been actualized, and the "news" as when the idea actually happens.

4 – ONLY INVEST WHAT YOU CAN LOSE

YOU Must Be Smart !!

Only invest what YOU know you can part with.

Anything can happen in the markets (and that means ANYTHING), so do NOT do anything foolish or greedy when it comes to YOUR risk exposure.

You may have heard of instances where people put their entire life savings into one stock or into the market, only to lose it all on a company bankruptcy or market downturn (ex., Enron, 2008 crash). Do yourself a favor and DIVERSIFY into different investments and sectors. You'll thank yourself in the long run if something goes wrong while your other things go right!

5 – QUESTION EVERYTHING

Question YOURSELF,
Question Others,
Be Objective!

YOU will learn quickly that being as objective as humanly possible will protect you from unnecessary losses and increase your

bottom line. Always ask YOURSELF, "What can go wrong in this trade?" and assess what you find.

Anyone you find who claims a "can't miss"

in a trading call has a blindspot, so you must analyze the trade and figure out what can go wrong. It's not that you and others are always wrong. This is done more so to prevent being blindsided and unnecessary losses.

Risk management is KEY to YOUR long term success, so protect your capital! Question YOURSELF, Question OTHERS, Question EVERYTHING!

6 – FOCUS ON BLUE CHIP COMPANIES

YOU are in GOOD Hands with Most Blue Chip Companies

Stocks on the Dow and S&P 500 are made to be the top performing stocks in the

United States stock market, as underperforming companies are cycled out for new upstarts delivering alpha.

Sure, you see IPO's and penny stocks, and new companies in new sectors that will be tomorrow's Amazon and Apple. Maybe focus a small percentage of your portfolio on these angel investments, while keeping your overall portfolio in companies with big balance sheets that routinely perform well at earnings.

7 - OVERBOUGHT AND OVERSOLD = GOLD

YOU LOVE Overbought and Oversold Conditions!

For you, the investor who's a bit more knowledgable on technical analysis (I teach you this in my stock market course!), you know a look at the RSI

indicator (relative strength index indicator) shows you when a stock is about to take a turn in the other direction.

Are you seeing a stock with a big run up and overbought? Time for YOU to take profits, open a short, or buy puts (if buying options) because a stock dip is imminent. A stock down in the dumps and oversold? Could be a great

buying opportunity short term, as a bounce in the stock price is imminent.

One of my favorite times to look at a stock is when the RSI hits overbought or oversold. This is one of the easiest trades you can find.

8 – LOOK FOR STOCKS WITH ROOM TO RUN

When YOU Have Room to Run, TAKE ACTION !!

Whether YOU have a stock that recently made a new high, but retraced the move, or YOU have a stock reversing out of a long term bear market with little to no resistances (I teach you about support & resistance in my stock course!), you always have a great opportunity when you see on your chart your stock has room to run to the upside.

Enjoy that smooth sailing and no resistances as your stock moves up to previously made highs and achieves new ones.

By the way, it's particularly fun seeing a stock in a long term bear market make new gains but still stay way off all time highs. That means YOU can go even further in its run UP!

9 – FOLLOW YOUR RULES AND STICK TO THEM

Stick to YOUR Script !!

Very Important! YOU see so many traders, especially new ones, jump off of their horse seeking a new bandwagon.

Yes, it is great for you to stay open-minded on other opportunities, but DON'T be foolish and abandon YOUR winning strategy overnight for something new and shiny.

If you are looking for the right strategy, then yes, you're more apt to hop around looking for one, but PLEASE find a strategy that works (I give YOU my strategies in my stock market course!). YOU need rules! Stick to your rules and your checklist in ALL of YOUR trades, because once you start making exceptions in YOUR rules, you're going down a path that can and WILL lose YOU money in the future.

10 – NEVER STOP LEARNING

YOU'RE in a GREAT PLACE !!

YOU LOVE all the new and exciting changes the market has to offer! New companies, new technologies, new financial instruments, and more! You always have new, fun things on the horizon in the markets, and just like with football, your favorite tv series, or MILK, the more up to date YOU are, the better!

YOU ARE in an amazing sport where all you have to do is use your brain to win and excel!

Warren Buffett (CEO of Berkshire Hathaway) is considered to be the best American investor in history, and he is STILL one of the best TODAY at 90 years young! You've got this! Enjoy the ride!

The market is waiting for you to earn your way to success! All you have to do is stay fresh, current, and up to date in your learning! I help YOU via my education courses online.

YOUR success in the market starts NOW.

GLOSSARY OF TERMS

Are YOU confused by a few words?

It's ALL good!

The market terminology you read and you hear can be confusing at times, but you just keep at it! You know I was once in your shoes, so please understand YOU are doing great!

If YOU can understand the names and terms in football, Real Housewives, ceramics, WWE, or any other specific field of interest, then YOU CAN get these terms too! You're amazing so don't be discouraged! Just enjoy your journey and stay on your path of learning :)

all time high. also known as a record high; the highest historical price level reached by a security, commodity, or index; measured from when instrument first starts trading and updates whenever last record high is exceeded.

angel investment. financial backing for small startups or entrepreneurs, typically in exchange for ownership equity in the company.

Apple. American multinational technology company headquartered in Cupertino, California, that designs, develops, and sells consumer electronics, computer software, and online services.

Amazon. American multinational technology company based in Seattle, Washington, which focuses on e-commerce, cloud computing, digital streaming, and artificial intelligence

balance sheet. a financial statement that provides a snapshot of what a company owns and owes, as well as the amount invested by shareholders.

bear market. when a market experiences prolonged price declines; typically describes a condition in which prices fall 20% or more from recent highs amid negative investor sentiment.

blue chip. a nationally recognized, well-established, financially sound company; company generally sells high-quality, widely accepted products and services; known to weather downturns, long record of stable and reliable growth.

bounce. a short-term correction where price goes up

bottom line. a company's earnings, profit, net income, or earnings per share; a company growing its earnings or reducing its costs is said to be improving its bottom line

"buy the rumor". a market adage based on belief stock prices move in anticipation of rumors and rebound when profit taking occurs after the actual news is released; investors buying an asset on potential news or information suggesting an asset may produce more future cash flows

capital. financial assets such as funds held in deposit accounts, brokerage accounts, and/or funds obtained from special financing sources

chart. graphical representation of an asset's historical price action

cycled out. market cycles, also known as stock market cycles, refers to trends or patterns that emerge during different markets or business environments; during a cycle, some securities or asset classes outperform others because their business models aligned with conditions for growth

delivering alpha. alpha is the excess return on an investment after adjusting for market-related volatility and random fluctuations.

diversify. diversification is a risk management strategy that mixes a wide variety of investments within a portfolio.

Dow. Dow Jones Industrial Average (DJIA), also known as the Dow 30, is a stock market index that tracks 30 large, publicly-owned blue-chip companies

downturn. A period of contraction or decline in economic activity

earnings. the amount of profit a company produces during a specific period, which is usually defined as a quarter (three calendar months) or a year.

evenly weighted. a type of weighting that gives same weight, or importance, to each stock in a portfolio.

financial instruments. assets that can be traded; can be cash, a contractual right to deliver or receive cash, or evidence of one's ownership of an entity.

investor. any person or entity who commits capital with expectation of receiving financial returns

IPO. An initial public offering refers to process of offering shares of a private corporation to the public in a new stock issuance; transition from a private to a public company; provides time for private investors to fully realize gains from their initial investment

overbought. a condition where an asset has traded at a level believed to be above its intrinsic or fair value; good candidate for sale

oversold. a condition where an asset has traded lower in price and has the potential for a price bounce.

penny stock. stock of a small company that trades for less than $5 per share

portfolio. collection of financial investments like stocks, bonds, commodities, cash, and cash equivalents

profits. financial benefit realized when revenue generated from a business activity exceeds the expenses, costs, and taxes involved in sustaining the activity in question

puts. an options contract that gives the owner the right, but not the obligation, to sell a certain amount of the underlying asset at a set price within a specific time; buyer of put option believes underlying stock will drop below exercise price before the expiration date

resistances. a resistance level, is the price at which the price of an asset meets pressure on its way up by emergence of growing number of sellers who wish to sell at that price.

retraced. temporary reversal of a trend in a stock's price.

risk. the chance an outcome or investment's actual gains will differ from an expected outcome; includes possibility of losing some or all of an original investment.

risk exposure. financial exposure is the amount an investor stands to lose in an investment should the investment fail; financial exposure, which is an alternative name for risk, is a crucial part of the investment process.

risk management. process of analysis and acceptance of uncertainty in investment decisions; occurs when an investor analyzes and attempts to quantify potential for losses in an investment

room to run. a run, in technical analysis, is a series of consecutive price movements that occur in the same direction; a run is constituted by a prolonged uptrend or downtrend, characterized by repeated daily gains or losses

RSI. relative strength index is a momentum indicator used in technical analysis; measures recent price changes to evaluate overbought or oversold conditions in the price of a stock or other asset.

S&P 500. Standard & Poor's 500 is an index of 500 of the largest publicly traded companies in the U.S.; widely regarded as the best gauge of U.S. stocks

sector. an area of economy or industry that shares common operating characteristics

"sell the news". a market adage based on belief stock prices move in anticipation of rumors and rebound when profit taking occurs after the actual news is released; investors selling an asset after actualized news event

short. a short position, is created when a trader sells a security first with intention of repurchasing it or covering it later at a lower price; trader may decide to short a security when believing the price of that security is likely to decrease in the near future.

"smart money". cash invested or wagered by those considered experienced, well informed, "in-the-know," or all three

stock. also known as equity; represents ownership of a fraction of a corporation; entitles owner to a proportion of the corporation's assets and profits equal to proportion of equity owned

technical analysis. a trading discipline employed to evaluate investments and identify trading opportunities by analyzing statistical trends gathered from trading activity, such as price movement and volume.

trade. a basic economic concept involving buying and selling of goods and services, with compensation paid by a buyer to a seller, or the exchange of goods or services between parties

trading call. a time when buyers set a maximum acceptable price to buy, and sellers set the minimum satisfactory price to sell on an exchange

upside. potential increase in value, measured in monetary or percentage terms, of an investment

ABOUT THE AUTHOR

Uch Anyanwu is an investor, educator, and a church-going, golf-loving international dj.

Born Uchenna Anyanwu in St. Vincent's Hospital, New York City, on August 30, 1979, Uch now resides in Las Vegas, Nevada USA and frequently weighs in on the markets throughout the online and social media landscape. You can find him teaching the stock market and cryptocurrency to students around the globe, with his students reaching all time highs, gaining expert knowledge about the markets, and making thousands of dollars in profits.

You can see his travels have landed him working partnerships in countries and cities around the world including Dubai, Ibiza, Los Angeles, Amsterdam, Barcelona, London, Berlin, Koh Samui, and Doha among others, further solidifying his masterful analysis of the global marketplace.

His dedication to God and his church family knows no bounds, serving as a Ministry Partner at Central Christian Church of Henderson, Nevada USA, including his weekly on-stage hosting of church services and playing piano for Central's Worship band Sunday mornings.

Having grown up in The Bronx, New York USA, the oldest child of seven, he and his siblings have achieved incredible heights, including 2 Emmy awards, New York Times write-ups, 2 medical school graduations, featured articles in Women's Wear Daily, multiple working collaborations alongside Grammy award winners & nominees, and tv production in all the major U.S. television networks to name a few. His parents, Martin and Cecilia Anyanwu were born in Nigeria and met in New York City, Cecilia being the child of a farmer and Martin being a United Nations diplomat on behalf of the Nigerian Mission.

INDEX

You are the Best YOU that was EVER Made

I Believe in YOU